AF615958

THE SABER-TOOTHED TIGER

THE SIBERIAN TIGER

by Jason M. Burns

Full Tilt Press
42964 Osgood Road
Fremont, CA 94539
readfulltilt.com
Full Tilt Press publications may be purchased for educational, business, or sales promotional use.

All internet sites appearing in back matter were available and accurate when this book was sent to press.

ISBN: 978-1-62920-766-7 (hardcover)

ISBN: 978-1-62920-790-2 (ePUB eBook)

ISBN: 978-1-62920-796-4 (PDF eBook)

Editorial Credits
Editor: Mari Bolte, Meghan Gottschall, and Michelle Parkin

Copyeditor: Kelley Barth

Designer: Sara Radka

Image Credits
page 3: ©Daniel Eskridge/Stocktrek Images / Getty Images; page 3: ©AlexTurton / Getty Images; page 3: ©Joe Giddens - PA Images / Contributor / Getty Images; page 3: ©Vac1 / Getty Images; page 7: ©Andyworks / Getty Images; page 8: ©Julia Mineeva/ZUMAPRESS / Newscom; page 8: ©Mark Kostich / Getty Images; page 9: ©Daniel Eskridge / Getty Images; page 10: ©msan10 / Getty Images; page 10: ©Alexey Yaremenko / Getty Images; page 11: ©estt / Getty Images; page 11: ©Galina Sinelnikova / Getty Images; page 12: ©CoreyFord / Getty Images; page 13: ©Gerard Lacz/NHPA/Photoshot / Newscom; page 14: ©Vac1 / Getty Images; page 16: ©John Conrad / Getty Images; page 17: ©Byrdyak / Getty Images; page 18: ©Elenarts108 / Getty Images; page 19: ©Mariomassone / Wikimedia; page 19: ©AlizadaStudios / Getty Images; page 19: ©Cropbot / Wikimedia; page 21: ©sduben / Getty Images; page 22: ©DIMITAR DILKOFF / Contributor / Getty Images; page 23: ©Keyur Nandaniya / Getty Images; page 24: ©Kevin Schafer / Getty Images; page 25: ©skynesher / Getty Images; page 27: ©guenterguni / Getty Images; page 27: ©Life On White / Getty Images; page 28: ©GlobalP / Getty Images

Cover: ©orinoco-art / Getty Images; ©Hatalskaya / Shutterstock; ©Chatchai Kittikun / Getty Images

Printed in the United States of America.

CONTENTS

INTRODUCTION

Imagine a cat as big as a grizzly bear. Its razor-sharp teeth glint in the moonlight. It lets out a deep growl that causes the hairs to prickle on the back of your neck. You are face-to-face with one of the most feared predators in the world.

We could be talking about the Siberian tiger. Or, if we lived thousands of years ago, we could just as easily be talking about the saber-toothed tiger.

Saber-toothed tigers disappeared long ago, but we can still learn a lot from them. What we learn can help save animals today that are at risk of disappearing forever. The Siberian tiger is one of those animals. Every day, it is one step closer to being lost to time.

Saber-Toothed Truths

Siberian tigers and saber-toothed tigers both have more than one name! Saber-toothed tigers are also called *Smilodons*. Siberian tigers are also known as Amur tigers.

CHAPTER 1

SMILING FELINES

Although saber-toothed tigers and Siberian tigers are not closely related, these fierce predators do share many similarities. One is their teeth.

Saber-toothed tigers are not closely related to tigers or modern cats.

Fangs aren't the only teeth in a tiger's mouth. In total, they have 30 teeth!

The saber-toothed tiger had two large fangs growing down from its upper jaw. These teeth could reach over 7 inches (17.8 centimeters) long. Imagine two pencils growing out of your face! The Siberian tiger also has large fangs. Even though they're smaller than the saber-toothed tiger's, they're still the longest **canine teeth** of any predator alive today.

canine tooth: the pointed tooth between the front and back teeth

Saber-toothed tigers lived throughout North and South America starting around 2.5 million years ago. They went **extinct** around 11,000 years ago. Scientists know a lot about these big cats because of the La Brea **Tar Pits** in California. More than a million bones belonging to 2,000 different *Smilodons* have been discovered there.

extinct: an entire species that has died off

tar pit: a hole where tar oozes out of the ground; tar traps animals and preserves their bones

New discoveries are being made every day at the La Brea Tar Pits.

THE BIGGER THEY ARE...

When diving into the past, one thing is clear—there were a lot of BIG animals. One was the dire wolf. This wolf is believed to be the biggest **canine** to have ever lived.

The dire wolf lived in North America and ran alongside gray wolves. Both species coexisted for thousands of years. Although they look and act similar, scientists believe they are not closely related. Dire wolves lived and hunted in **packs**. They ate wild horses and ground sloths. Gray wolves live and hunt in family groups too. Deer, elk, and bison are their biggest prey.

Dire wolves disappeared around the same time as the *Smilodon*. Scientists still aren't sure why they died out when the gray wolf survived.

canine: a member of the dog family

pack: a group of wild animals that live and hunt together

In movies, saber-toothed tigers are often shown as giant monsters. In fact, they were slightly smaller than modern lions! But they were still huge, standing at 3 feet (0.9 meters) tall and 6 feet (1.8 m) long. And they were twice as heavy as the lion, weighing as much as 620 pounds (281.2 kilograms).

Siberian tigers are even bigger. They stand 3.5 feet (1 m) tall at the shoulder and can grow up to 12 feet (3.7 m) long. They can weigh up to 660 pounds (299.4 kg). They are fast too, reaching speeds of up to 60 miles (96.6 kilometers) per hour.

MEASURING UP

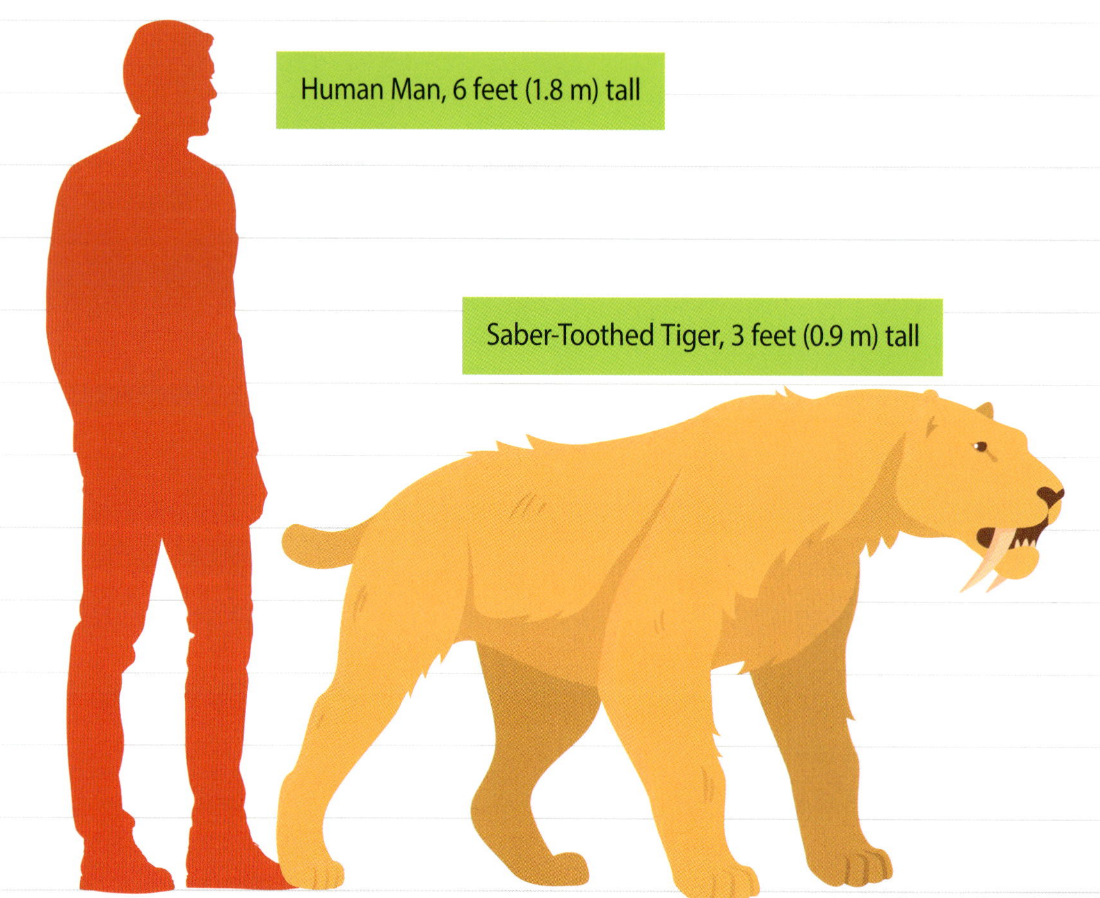

Smilodon means "knife tooth."

Siberian Tiger, 3.5 feet (1 m) tall

Scientists believe that the saber-toothed tiger was a pack animal. They hunted large prey like bison and woolly mammoths. Pack hunting makes it easier to bring down prey. Lions are another big cat species that hunt together.

Siberian tigers are **solitary** hunters. Their striped coats help them blend in as they sneak up on prey. They eat animals like elk and wild boar. Hunting alone means not having to share the prize. A Siberian tiger can eat more than 60 pounds (27.2 kg) of food in one sitting.

solitary: alone

Saber-toothed tigers would have hunted herbivores, similar to the deerlike *Kyptoceras*.

Wild boars are tough creatures, but Siberian tigers are more than a match for them.

CHAPTER 2

BIG CATS, SHRINKING POPULATIONS

While saber-toothed tigers are related to modern cats, they have no living **descendants**. They first appeared around 2.5 million years ago. They disappeared close to 10,000 years ago. No one knows why. Scientists think that when their food died out, the saber-toothed tiger did too.

The first *Smilodon* fossils were found in the 1830s.

descendant: originating from a common ancestor

All tigers are rare. There are only around 3,500 to 5,500 tigers left in the wild.

There is only one kind of tiger alive today. They are divided into six different groups. Three other groups have gone extinct. The divisions began recently, about 20,000 years ago. Tigers belonging to different groups can mate and raise cubs together. Some experts think this is a good idea. It will help add **genetic diversity**. Others are against it. They think each group should stay as pure as possible.

genetic diversity: the range of genetic characteristics or traits within a species

BACK FROM THE BRINK

The North American gray wolf is the largest living canine species. Back when the United States was young, around 2 million wolves roamed the land. But by the early 1900s, they were nearly hunted to extinction. Farmers felt the wolves threatened their families and livestock. They wanted to rid their land of the predators. Others wanted wolf furs to sell or trade. At one point, there were only 300 wolves left.

In the 1960s, the gray wolf fell under government protection. It became illegal to hunt or harm them. Wolf populations began to bounce back. There are now thousands of wild wolves. **Conservation** efforts have made a huge impact on keeping wolves around for future generations.

conservation: the protection of animals and plants

Today, the saber-toothed tiger is extinct. Siberian tigers are still around, but their numbers are dwindling. If they disappear too, the whole environment will change. Tigers are **apex predators**. They control the number of prey species in an area. Sick animals are usually removed by predators. Without predators, prey can become overpopulated. When overpopulation happens, disease and other illnesses spread quickly.

Plants in the area might never recover if prey animals become overpopulated. There might not be enough water to go around. Space is an issue too. Deer, rodents, and other prey animals will spill over into places where humans live.

apex predator: at the top of the food chain

Climate change, habitat loss, and rising sea levels are only a few of the threats to Siberian tigers.

Facing extinction means **adapting** or dying out. Tigers **evolved** from miacids. These small carnivorous mammals began to change 65 million years ago, after the dinosaur extinction. They ranged in size from house cats to wolves. Scientists believe they lived at least part-time in trees. All modern carnivores, including *Smilodons* and tigers, can trace their roots back to miacids. Miacids were able to thrive after dinosaurs went extinct. Mammals like miacids no longer had to hide during the day to avoid predators.

adapt: to adjust to new conditions

evolve: to develop over time

Saber-Toothed Truths

For millions of years, mammals and dinosaurs lived together. Dinosaurs were huge. Mammals were smaller. The largest was about the size of a raccoon. After dinosaurs went extinct, mammals began to thrive. They split off into different species. They grew in size thanks to a warmer planet, less competition, and fewer predators. Mammals took over the areas where dinosaurs once lived. Some of those mammals evolved into humans. If the dinosaurs had been able to adapt, our world might be much different.

Purgatorius was a type of early primate.

Small carnivores evolved from miacids and into more modern-day predators.

Ancient carnivores started out small, but they were fast and fierce.

Over time, carnivores grew in size and strength.

CHAPTER 3

SHARING A SMALL SPACE

Modern humans have only been on the planet for about 200,000 years. Tigers have been on the planet 10 times longer than that. We have never known a world without tigers.

When people and big cats share space, accidents happen. A herd of cattle or sheep is an easy meal for a tiger. Sometimes people get in the way. Humans also cut down forests for fuel and farmland. Siberian tigers used to live throughout eastern Asia. They have lost much of their original habitat.

Tigers must travel hundreds of miles to find food and mates. Habitat loss makes that trek even harder.

As human populations continue to spread, forests are torn down. The animals who live there, including tigers, have less space. Because tigers are solitary creatures, they require their own space. Female tigers have home territories around 7.7 square miles (20 square kilometers). Males have an even larger range. And males must be able to travel between territories to mate. **Deforestation** breaks up the territories. When it is hard, or even impossible, to travel between them, tiger populations struggle.

deforestation: the loss of forests

Deforestation removes acorns and pine nuts from the forest. This is the main food supply for the animals Siberian tigers eat.

Since the beginning of the 1900s, around 97 percent of all the world's tigers have been lost.

Tigers have lived for millions of years without humans getting involved. But once humans entered the picture, the future of tigers became unclear. Siberian tigers are classified as endangered. This means they face a high risk of extinction in the future.

It is estimated that there are only about 400 Siberian tigers left in the wild. Between 20 and 30 are killed every year by poachers. The tigers' fur, teeth, bones, and other body parts are sold illegally for medicine or trophies.

Tigers have no natural predators. Their only threat is people.

CREATIVE CONSERVATION

Sometimes scientists must get creative to save a species or **ecosystem**. The World Wildlife Fund (WWF) is leading the way. Their work saving Kenya's lions could change how big cats are valued and taken care of.

The WWF has installed hundreds of solar-powered lights on Kenyan farms. These lights turn on and flicker when a lion gets too close. The lion thinks a person is nearby, and they run off. The lights help keep the lions safe and protect the farm's livestock and workers.

ecosystem: all the living things that live inside an environment

When the planet began to warm up, many animals could not adapt. Prey died, and big cats starved. They had to compete with early humans for food too.

But people can help tigers thrive today. Scientists are keeping track of populations. Conservationists are also doing their part. There are more than 500 Siberian tigers in **captivity**. Zoos, sanctuaries, and breeding centers are trying to encourage captive tigers to reproduce. Their goal is to send captive-bred tigers to live in the wild.

Laws protect tigers. Activists fight against poaching and deforestation. Without human interference, tigers could be extinct within the next 20 years. *Smilodon* may be gone forever, but with education and conservation, Siberian tigers can be here for years to come.

captivity: living under human care or control

There are around 5,000 tigers in captivity in the United States.

PREHISTORIC MAINSTAYS

Did you know that there are many prehistoric species still alive today? Okapis are called living fossils. That means they haven't changed much, or at all, for millions of years. Okapis are only found in the Democratic Republic of Congo. The okapi is a shy creature. It was not documented by Europeans until 1901. They thought okapis were forest unicorns.

The okapi's closest living relative is the giraffe. No one knows how many okapis are left in the world, but it is estimated that there are less than 5,000. They are considered endangered.

QUIZ

1 Another name for the Siberian tiger is:

a. saber-toothed tiger
b. Amur tiger
c. saber-toothed cat
d. smiling tiger

2 True or false: Mammals and dinosaurs lived at the same time.

a. true
b. false

3 Siberian tigers are ______.

a. extinct
b. vulnerable
c. threatened
d. endangered

4 Animals that have been around for millions of years but haven't changed much over time are called:

a. dinosaurs
b. living fossils
c. crocodilian
d. mammalian

Key: 1) b; 2) b; 3) d; 4) b

ACTIVITY

GLOW AND TELL

Have you ever noticed how a cat's eyes seem to glow in the dark? A tiger's eyes work the same way. But why? This easy—and fun!—experiment will shed a little light on the subject.

WHAT YOU NEED

- scissors
- ruler
- black garbage bag
- empty aluminum can with one end removed
- rubber band
- flashlight

STEPS TO TAKE

1. Ask an adult to cut an 8-inch (20.3 centimeters) circle from the trash bag.
2. Then carefully cut a 1-inch (2.5 cm) oval in the center of the plastic piece. The hole should be about the size of your eye.
3. Wrap the plastic piece over a short side of the can. Use the rubber band to hold the plastic in place. Center the oval.
4. Shut off all the lights in the room. Make sure it is dark!
5. Shine the flashlight into the opening in the can. Can you see a glow? The light is reflecting off the back of the can. This is the same science behind how a cat's eyes glow in the dark.

GLOSSARY

adapt *(uh-DAPT)*: to adjust to new conditions

apex predator *(AY-peks PRED-uh-tuhr)*: at the top of the food chain

canine *(KAY-nine)*: a member of the dog family

canine tooth *(KAY-nine TOOTH)*: the pointed tooth between the front and back teeth

captivity *(kap-TIV-uh-tee)*: living under human care or control

conservation *(kon-sur-VAY-shuhn)*: the protection of animals and plants

deforestation *(DEE-for-uh-STAY-shuhn)*: the loss of forests

descendant *(duh-SEN-duhnt)*: originating from a common ancestor

ecosystem *(EE-koh-sys-tuhm)*: all the living things that live inside an environment

evolve *(uh-VOLV)*: to develop over time

extinct *(ik-STINGKT)*: an entire species that has died off

genetic diversity *(juh-NET-ik dye-VUR-suh-tee)*: the range of genetic characteristics or traits within a species

pack *(PAK)*: a group of wild animals that live and hunt together

solitary *(SAH-luh-teh-ree)*: alone

tar pit *(TAR PIT)*: a hole where tar oozes out of the ground; tar traps animals and preserves their bones

READ MORE

Eason, Katherine. *Big Cats: And Their Food Chains.* Minneapolis, MN: Cheriton Children's Books, 2023.

Hirsch, Rebecca E. *Living Fossils: Survivors from Earth's Distant Past.* Minneapolis, MN: Millbrook Press, 2021.

INTERNET SITES

Suiting Up for Smilodon
https://tarpits.org/stories/suiting-smilodon
See a lifelike creation of a Smilodon from the La Brea Tar Pits & Museum.

Trail Cam Captures Footage of Extremely Rare Siberian Tiger
https://outsider.com/outdoors/trail-cam-captures-footage-of-extremely-rare-siberian-tiger/
See a Siberian tiger in its natural habitat.

INDEX